ELEPHANT THEORY

HOW OUR SUBCONSCIOUS MORALITY DRIVES POLITICS, CULTURE, AND CIVILIZATION

D.M. NORDMARK

CONTENTS

INTRODUCTION

> *It is not the strongest of the species that survive, nor the most intelligent, but the one most responsive to change.* – **Charles Darwin**

Through the process of natural selection, evolution shapes and moulds every life form on Earth. Those organisms which exhibit traits that are better suited to the environment, whether they be plant, insect or animal, are more likely to survive and reproduce. Over generations, these advantageous traits will often become so common to the point that new species can develop. This dynamic is what drives biodiversity, influences ecosystems, and results in the variety of life forms we see on Earth today.

Evolution not only affects physical structures such as a giraffe's long neck or the chameleon's ability to blend into the environment, but behaviour as well. Pacific salmon must return to the stream from which they were hatched.

Male bowerbirds build incredibly complex structures in order to attract a mate. Monarch butterflies return to central Mexico in order to breed. If you were to ask a person why these animals do this, the answer most likely would be "instinct," which is true. However, these instincts and behaviours were forged in the fires of evolution as well.

Human Beings like to think they are different, however, as we have reason. Unlike other animals in nature, we have the ability to conceptualize ideas and perceive how they may be used in the future. We like to think that we are not governed by unthinking instinct like Salmon or Bowerbirds for we are logical beings. We do not act due to unthinking instinct, but reason. That's what we like to tell ourselves, at any rate. The only problem is that it's wrong.

The truth is that what we perceive as thinking is largely an illusion. Our actions are guided by evolutionary instinct just as much as any animal or insect. *Man is not a rational animal; he is a rationalizing animal,* notes science fiction legend Robert Heinlein, and he is correct. As I write this in May of 2024, it may feel that the world is coming unhinged. From the COVID panic to the rise of Donald Trump to the collapse of Hollywood, there doesn't seem to be a major institution that isn't causing strife, perplexing people, or falling apart. On the surface, pundits will try to rationalize various political and social theories for why this is occurring, but they are just that, surface-level. If you really want to understand what is going on and why, you need to look below our perceived rationalizations and understand the evolutionary reasons for our political divides. To the uninitiated, reason and logic can appear like the great and powerful Oz. The reality, though, is that the person who is really pulling the strings is evolution and instinct, not reason. Why is the Pacific salmon compelled to return to the stream from which it spawned? Evolutionary instinct. Why do male bowerbirds build their impressive structures? Instinct. Why are right-leaning people seemingly much less progressive on issues such as gay marriage? Instinct. Our big brains do allow us to build atomic bombs and mint toothpaste. However, when it comes to how we behave, we are not so different from our animal cousins at all.

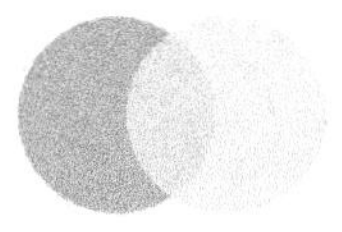

EVOLUTION

Nothing in biology makes sense except in the light of evolution. – **Theodosius Dobzhansky**

The goal of all life on Earth is to survive and procreate. From the time man's ancestors first emerged from the ocean, crawling onto the beach as muddy fish, this was accomplished by what we would call instinct, or the instinct to survive. The evolutionary path we followed looks roughly like this:

Aquatic Ancestors - This is the fish that started it all. Our aquatic ancestors were most likely some kind of lungfish which could breathe air and had limb-like fins.

Early Tetrapods - Comparable to modern-day amphibians, these creatures were comfortable living both on land and in water.

Reptile-like Synapsids - Comparable to modern-day reptiles, these creatures evolved into an animal with a mix of mammalian and reptilian features.

Small Mammals - Comparable to modern-day mice or shrews, these early mammals were small and nocturnal.

Primates - Comparable to modern-day lemurs, these early primates were tree-dwellers with grasping hands. They also began to live in social groups for the purposes of raising young, finding food, and protection from predators.

Great Apes - Comparable to modern-day chimpanzees or bonobos, these are our closest living relatives.

Early Humans - There are no modern equivalents of early humans. These ancestors were like "Lucy" (scientifically known as Australopithecines). These early humans could walk upright but retained ape-like features.

Modern Humans - Modern humans are characterized by being largely hairless with advanced tool use, language, and complex societies.

There are three watershed moments in the evolutionary history I've listed here, but most people only recognize the significance of two of them. These are when that fish first walked on land and when man began using tools. The reality is that the second overlooked event, namely living in groups, had just as much impact on who we are today, if not more so, than the other two.

This is our evolutionary tree, and what it shows is that for most of our history, our ancestors have relied on instinct to survive. During this time, our biological adaptations, such as becoming air breathers or giving birth to live young, were mainly physical. This began to change once we reached the primate/great ape stage when we began to live in groups. Living in groups provides tremendous evolutionary benefits in terms of survival, but it also requires new behaviours in terms of group dynamics. Certain behaviours work well in groups, whereas others do not. This is the evolutionary root of our morality, or codes of conduct on how we treat each other. This is why basic moral thoughts, such as "thou shall not kill," are an outgrowth of evolution. This moral programming became a second layer in our mind, serving our primal instincts of survival and procreation.

The final major addition to our survival mind occurred when our ape ancestors began to use simple tools. This action required the emergence of abstract thinking and foresight. There are tremendous evolutionary advantages to being able to think this way, and this ability evolved quickly on an evolutionary scale. This stage in the evolution of our mind laid the foundation for advanced cognitive functions such as language, culture, and technology. It is this evolution of the mind that made us who we are today.

The important point here is that our ability to think rationally was the last layer to be added to the conditional structures of our procreation computer, otherwise known as the human brain. This is why we are fooled into thinking that we are ruled by reason, but in reality, reason is always subservient to the operations of the first two.

THE HUMAN COMPUTER

The human brain is a kludge of adaptations from different periods of evolutionary history that happens to be able to build computers.
— **Eliezer Yudkowsky**

In order to understand human behaviour we need to understand how our evolutionary programming works. Like all animals, all aspects of human evolution, both physical and mental, have developed for the purpose of ensuring our survival so we can procreate. From the previous section we can see that our mind has gone through three major evolutionary stages. If we were to conceive of our brain as a biological computer, it would look something like this:

- **Primal Instinct Layer** - This is the foundational layer of our brain's intelligence stack and has been with us even before our fish ancestors first crawled out of the ocean over 400 million years ago. This layer manifests itself in our most powerful drives, such as our will to survive and desire to reproduce.

- **Group Morality Layer** - This layer was added on top of our primal instinct layer about 65 million years ago when we began to live in social groups as primates. This evolutionary step manifests itself in our morality, the code of conduct by which we treat each other.

- **Logic Reason Layer** - This is the most recent addition to our brain's intelligence stack and is therefore the least powerful. This bit of code was added about 3 million years ago when our ancestors began to use tools. This is the layer that man has developed beyond any other animal and allows us to dominate the world. It gives us the power to create modern societies and everything in them, from selfie sticks to space shuttles. As this layer gives us such unique abilities, it is easy to fall into the trap of thinking it separates us from the rest of the animal kingdom. Man is guided by reason and logic, whereas animals are driven by instinct. This is an illusion. Our logic layer only reigns supreme when it is working independently of our two base layers. You are rational when you are doing something that doesn't involve emotion, like buying gas for your car.

Very few of our decisions are emotion-free, however, which is why we are just as instinctive and irrational as our animal brethren 90% of the time.

The Logic Reason Tier is usually completely unaware of how the lower levels are operating and why they are doing what they are doing. The whole point of this little book is to give you some insight into why the man behind the curtain behaves as he does. We will now explore the Group Morality Tier of our biological computer brain. Once you understand this, you will understand why Conservative and Liberal Elephants "think" the way they do. It all comes down to whether they prioritize the success of their own herds or openness to others.

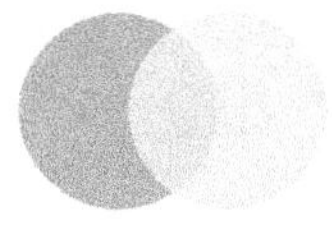

ELEPHANT THEORY

The mind is divided, like a rider on an elephant, and the rider's job is to serve the elephant.
— Jonathan Haidt

In his book *The Righteous Mind*, Jonathan Haidt compares the way the human brain works to that of a giant elephant ridden by a tiny rational rider. The elephant represents the first two stacks of our evolutionary programming—the instinctive and group layers—whereas the rider represents the recent addition of reason. The rational rider thinks he is in charge, but the reality is that the elephant is the one making the decisions. It is the elephant that decides the job you take, who you marry, and the kind of car you drive. The only thing the rider does is rationalize those decisions after the fact. The truth is that the rider is so irrelevant that I will scarcely mention him for the rest of this book. What counts is understanding our elephant drives and how they influence our decisions. This is the basis of our political disagreements, not reason or political theories. As we shall soon see, all of those highfalutin concepts are little more than rationalizations conjured up by our largely irrelevant rider.

Let's get back to our elephants. Once our ancestors began to live in social groups (as primates, but I will be using elephants as a stand-in from now on), our elephants were forced to make an evolutionary choice. How open would they be to elephants from other herds versus their own? One evolutionary strain found it advantageous to focus on the success of their own herd. The advantage of this is that if their own herd is successful, then they and their offspring are likely to be successful as well. However, at the same time, a second strain evolved that found it advantageous to be open to elephants from other herds. The evolutionary advantage of this is that accepting elephants outside of your herd increases the genetic diversity of your own. The first approach is the basis for the political leanings of conservative elephants, while the second guides the liberal variety. Let's now explore each of these evolutionary strategies in depth and how they manifest themselves in political philosophies and policies.

CONSERVATIVE ELEPHANTS

*The evolutionary path Conservative Elephants
followed causes them to focus on the social capital
and health of their immediate herd.*

Conservative Elephants followed the evolutionary path of focusing on building and supporting their own herds. Moral values and behaviours that supported this view were developed while those that weakened the herd were discouraged. In *The Righteous Mind,* Jonathan Haidt identifies six moral values [Code of Behaviours] that evolved to ensure optimal group dynamics. They are as follows:

Care/Harm - If your herd is to survive, you must ensure that your fellow elephants are protected, particularly the young. This moral value makes us sensitive to those in need and who may be suffering.

Liberty/Oppression - Successful herds require social structures and leaders. However, what if the herd's leaders take advantage of the social structures to benefit themselves while oppressing the rest of the herd? This instinct evolved so that smaller and weaker elephants can join together to overthrow systems and leaders that attempt to exploit the herd.

Fairness/Cheating - This moral evolved around the adaptive challenge of reaping the rewards of living in a herd without getting exploited. When everyone is contributing to the herd, the herd thrives. Elephants that actively avoid work and seek to only live off the efforts of others will build resentment, endangering the integrity of the herd. It only takes one bad apple to ruin the bunch.

Loyalty/Betrayal - This moral value evolved in order to maintain the integrity of the group and is similar to fairness/cheating. Having elephants that are team players and work to support the herd is important. If you are loyal to others, you expect them to be loyal to you. This moral value is a form of reciprocity. It makes us innately want to reward and trust loyal people while ostracizing those who betray that trust.

Authority/Subversion - This moral value evolved as large herds need some kind of organization to function, which manifests itself in forms of social hierarchies. This value reflects the fact that respecting established authority, traditions, and values—values that have developed with the wisdom of time—promote the stability of the herd.

Sanctity/Degradation - This moral value likely evolved due to the fact that for a herd to prosper, certain things need to be revered and seen as sacred; given special care, if you will. The protection of women and children can be seen in this light. Religious practices around the sanctity of marriage, sexual purity, and the innocence of childhood are examples of this. As they prevent disease and illness, restrictions around alcohol and drugs, as well as how food is prepared, are also results of this value. Life itself is seen as sacred, which is why abortion is opposed and suicide is a sin. Spaces themselves can be seen as sacred, as believing in a God or something that is beyond the individual can bring unity to a herd.

The evolutionary path that Conservative Elephants followed, that of focusing on their own herd, compels them to find merit in all six of Haidt's moral values. Visually, the moral matrix that Conservative Elephants see as important looks something like this:

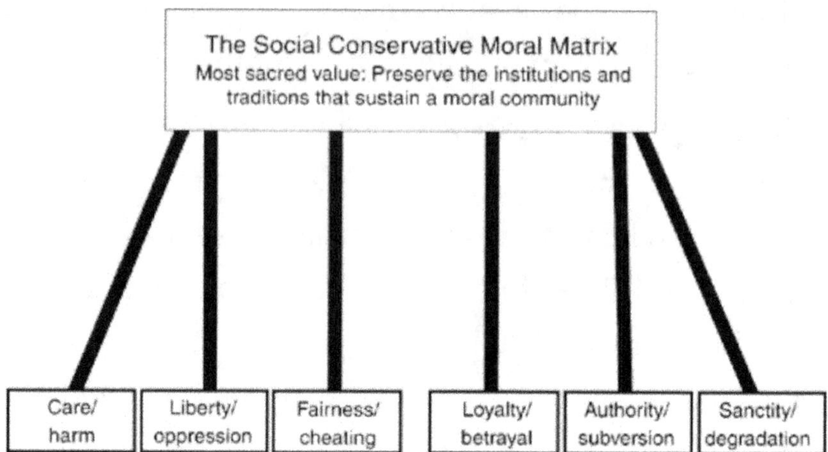
The Social Conservative Moral Matrix
Most sacred value: Preserve the institutions and
traditions that sustain a moral community
Care/
harm
Liberty/
oppression
Fairness/
cheating
Loyalty/
betrayal
Authority/
subversion
Sanctity/
degradation

THE CONSTRAINED VISION

The constrained vision takes human nature as given, and sees social outcomes as a function of the incentives presented to individuals and the conditions under which they interact in response to those incentives. — **Thomas Sowell**

The reality that elephants are not the same or inherently good leads Conservative Elephants to have what Thomas Sowell calls the constrained view of human nature. This political philosophy recognizes that elephant (and human) nature is inherently selfish and unchanging. As we are flawed beings, it emphasizes the importance of systemic processes, traditions, and checks and balances that have stood the test of time to restrain those flaws. Conservative Elephants know that forming a successful herd with strong social capital is difficult to achieve and maintain. Therefore, any changes to the structure of the herd should be made slowly and with great care. Those with the constrained vision recognize the limits of their own knowledge with respect to the wisdom of the past. They favour empirical evidence and practical approaches, acknowledging that in the real world, there are no perfect solutions—there are tradeoffs. Let's now look at how subscribing to the constrained vision causes Conservative Elephants to respond with policies through the lens of Haidt's six moral foundations.

CARE/HARM

National Defense - Conservative Elephants believe in a strong national defense to protect the herd. They are also wary of other herds who may present as threats.

Traditional Family Values - Conservative Elephants value traditional family structures as providing stable and caring environments for children as being tested and time proven. They are likely to support policies that strengthen this aspect of the social fabric.

Law and Order - Conservative Elephants are more likely to focus on strict law enforcement to protect the herd from the criminal element within it. As they see all elephants as potentially being flawed, they are more likely to place the blame on individual bad actors rather than any system that may have created it.

FAIRNESS/CHEATING

Meritocracy - Conservative Elephants accept that elephants in their herds are not the same in either abilities or the effort they undertake. This is why they are more likely to accept the reality of unequal outcomes. Although they are aware of how systems can result in unequal outcomes, they tend to emphasize individual responsibility and merit. Opposition to affirmative action is an example of this. They instinctively are concerned with how such systems may promote unqualified candidates at the expense of the competency and social cohesion of the herd.

Law and Order - As Conservative Elephants see their natures as inherently flawed, they recognize that some elephants will try to take advantage of the herd. They therefore focus on laws that will protect the herd from bad actors. They want laws to be applied fairly and consistently based on the individual's actions. The representation of Lady Justice being blindfolded is a representation of this conservative idea.

Personal Accountability - Conservative Elephants believe that individuals are responsible for their actions first and foremost and are less likely to accept excuses due to external factors. As they see elephant nature as flawed they are constantly vigilant for those who would take advantage of the herd. This is why they are inherently skeptical of social programs that they fear may be taken advantage of by the unscrupulous and that might encourage dependency.

LIBERTY/OPPRESSION

Economic Liberties - Conservative Elephants believe in individual initiative and therefore value the maximum amount of economic freedom to allow for innovation.

Gun Rights - Conservative Elephants believe that individuals should be able to defend themselves. They believe in the power of individual action both in terms of responsibility and to resist oppression, including from the government.

Religious Freedom - Conservative Elephants emphasize the importance of protecting religious practices, particularly when those practices have been part of the spontaneous order that has contributed to the herd's success overtime. Conservative Elephants also value religious freedom as a means of unifying chaotic herds.

LOYALTY/BETRAYAL

Family, Community, Nation - As Conservative Elephants are focused on their herds and the flawed elephants that inhabit them, their loyalty is primarily directed from the bottom up. They are loyal first to family, then to community, and finally, to the nation. They are cautious about extending that loyalty to organizations beyond the national level, as they are wary of other elephant herds.

AUTHORITY/SUBVERSION

Law and Order - Conservative Elephants are more likely to believe in the rule of law and the institutions that support it. This is why Conservative Elephants, under normal circumstances, are more likely to "back the blue."

Support Traditional Values - Conservative Elephants are much more likely to support traditions and customs that have evolved over time, such as traditional family structures, religious practices, and national heritage.

SANCTITY/DEGRADATION

Sanctity Of Marriage - Conservative Elephants see marriage as being sacred as it is a time-tested institution that helps to preserve the social fabric of the herd. This is why they promote sexual purity, such as no sex before marriage, as they see sex as being an extremely powerful force that needs to be channeled and controlled.

Sanctity of Children - Raising successful children is crucial for the survival of the herd. Children are viewed as sacred and in need of protection from exposure to the adult world. This is why Conservative Elephants strongly oppose activities like drag queen story hour, as they consider such events to belong to the adult space—similar to strippers and pornography—and believe they should not be introduced to children.

Sanctity of Motherhood - The hand that rocks the cradle rules the world. Motherhood is seen as sacred as the raising of children to adulthood is so vital to the success of the herd. This is why Conservative Elephants see life itself as sacred and are much more likely to oppose abortion.

Body Integrity - Conservative Elephants are much more likely to keep the body pure and oppose practices such as tattoos or using substances that are seen to contaminate the body either physically or spiritually.

LIBERAL ELEPHANTS

The evolutionary path Liberal Elephants pursued caused them to be extremely open to elephants from other herds in order to benefit from genetic diversity.

Genetic diversity is crucial to the long-term survival of a population. Resistance to disease, a reduced chance of inbreeding, and greater adaptability to environmental changes are some of the advantages that genetically diverse herds enjoy. This is why Liberal Elephants evolved to be so open to individuals from other herds joining their own. However, this openness comes at a cost. Liberal Elephants must downplay those moral values related to the social cohesion of their own herd. This compels them to take the existing social order for granted and view the entire species as equal and inherently good. Failing to see their fellow elephants in this way would undermine their openness to elephants from other herds. This is why they prioritize only three of Jonathan Haidt's six moral values.

These are the three moral values that Liberal Elephants are able to value, as they do not hinder their primary evolutionary drive of openness.

Care/Harm - What differentiates Liberal Elephants from their Conservative brethren on this value is that Liberal Elephants are much more likely to express concern for elephants in herds other than their own.

Liberty/Oppression - Liberal Elephants are much more likely to view this moral value in terms of top-down systemic oppression of those they see as marginalized groups.

Fairness/Cheating - Liberal Elephants view this value in terms of groups they feel are being oppressed. They are less likely to factor in individual responsibility, as this would conflict with their belief that all elephants are the same and good. Therefore, when they see inequality, it must be the fault of an oppressive system rather than individual action. This also leads them to promote policies that encourage equal outcomes.

The following moral values, as they promote herd cohesion, are ignored by Liberal Elephants. Evolutionarily, this is because recognizing these values would make them less open to elephants from other herds.

Loyalty/Betrayal - Liberal Elephants express this moral in terms of universal values that can be applied to all. They are less likely to express greater loyalty to their own herd than to others.

Authority/Subversion - Liberal Elephants tend to reject this moral as they are suspicious of existing hierarchies and instinctively see them as sources of oppression. They also see existing social hierarchies as barriers to accepting elephants from other herds whose social hierarchies may not be compatible.

Sanctity/Degradation - Liberal Elephants place much less emphasis on this moral value and will only express it in universal terms. This is why environmental issues seen as global, such as "global warming" or valuing "mother Earth," are stressed.

The evolutionary path that Liberal Elephants followed, that of being open to elephants from other herds, compels them to find merit in only three of Haidt's six moral values. Visually, their moral matrix looks like this.

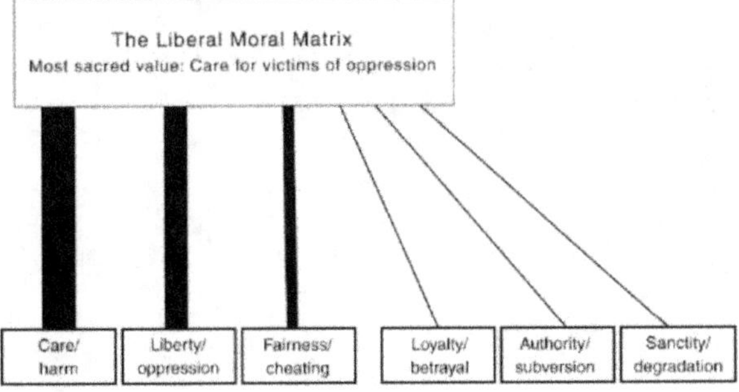

THE UNCONSTRAINED VISION OF LIBERAL ELEPHANTS

In the unconstrained vision, human nature itself is a variable, and in fact is the central variable to be changed. – **Thomas Sowell**

The evolutionary adaptation of being open to other herds led Liberal Elephants to view their nature as inherently good and malleable. This perspective is what Thomas Sowell refers to as the Unconstrained Vision of human (and elephant) nature. Why wouldn't you be open to others if you believe that elephant nature is inherently good? There's only upside if this is true. In cases where elephants are not behaving well, Liberal Elephants are confident in their ability to change the systems they believe are causing the issue. The Liberal Elephant philosopher Jean-Jacques Rousseau captured this idea with the phrase, "Man is born free, and everywhere he is in chains." Liberal

Elephants believe they can remove these systemic chains so that all can thrive. This belief leads them to favour top-down, transformative social policies, which they are confident they can implement and control. This is why Liberal Elephants are comfortable wielding government power and why they see issues in terms of problems and solutions, rather than trade-offs. When Conservative Elephants raise objections to their plans, rooted in the three moral values their unconstrained nature does not recognize (loyalty/betrayal, authority/subversion, sanctity/degradation), Liberal Elephants often cannot comprehend it. It's like asking a person with black-and-white vision to see colour. Their focused moral matrix makes it difficult for them to understand how others can look at the same data and yet reach different conclusions. Now, let's explore how subscribing to the Unconstrained Vision leads Liberal Elephants to advocate for various policies.

CARE/HARM

Universal Values - Liberal Elephants are much more likely to offer support for victims they have no relation to, such as saving Darfur or freeing Tibet. They are also more likely to support causes like animal rights.

Social Safety Nets - Liberal Elephants are much more likely to advocate for universal social safety nets such as universal health care or welfare. Further, they are likely to oppose any form of means testing for such programs.

Criminal Justice Reform - Liberal Elephants are much more likely to place emphasis on rehabilitation over punishment.

FAIRNESS /CHEATING

Equal Economic Outcomes - Liberal Elephants are much more likely to support policies that they think will lead to equal economic outcomes such as progressive income taxes and social programs.

Social Justice - As Liberal Elephants view all inequality as the result of oppressive systems, they are much more likely to advocate for programs like affirmative action to address it.

Corporate Accountability - Under normal circumstances Liberal Elephants are much more likely to be skeptical of corporate power and favour regulations to curb it.

LIBERTY/OPPRESSION

Civil Rights Movements - Liberal Elephants are much more likely to champion the causes of groups they see as victims of systemic oppression. Examples of this are Black Lives Matter and LGBTQ+ rights.

Social Programs - Liberal Elephants view poverty as an unnatural and oppressive system and therefore advocate for social programs to alleviate it.

As their primary evolutionary impulse is to be open and accepting of others, Liberal Elephants must discount or ignore the following three morals. To the extent they do recognize them, they are typically related to the previous three in some way.

LOYALTY/BETRAYAL

Global Solidarity - Liberal Elephants are much more likely to express support for agreements that go beyond their herds, such as the Paris Climate Accords and global human rights initiatives. This allows them to show loyalty to humanity as a whole which is compatible with their evolutionary outlook.

AUTHORITY/SUBVERSION

Critical of Authority - Liberal Elephants are much more skeptical of existing power structures as they are seen as impediments to openness. This is why they are so supportive of movements which challenge authority such as protests against the police or for greater civil rights.

Challenging Traditional Institutions and Values - Liberal Elephants are more likely to see traditional values and institutions as relics of the past, particularly if they enforce a hierarchy in any way. This is why they advocate for reforms in institutions like the church or the military to make them more open and less exclusionary and rules-based.

SANCTITY/DEGRADATION

Environmental Conservation - Liberal Elephants will tend to express this value in holistic terms such as the sanctity of the Earth. Taken to an extreme, they can see the environment as being so sacred that they are resistant to man exploiting it in any way. This is an outgrowth of the fact that they take the social fabric, in this case represented by civilization itself, for granted.

Sexual Morality - Liberal Elephants are much more accepting of issues like premarital sex, homosexuality and pornography. They see resistance to these ideas as being rooted in existing oppressive power structures that impairs openness to others.

Acceptance of Diverse Lifestyles - Liberal Elephants are more accepting of LGBTQ+ rights and non-traditional family structures as they see them as legitimate expressions of individual identity. The openness of Liberal Elephants compels them to accept the lifestyles of all individuals as being equal and good.

Support for Reproductive Rights - Liberal Elephants are more likely to support access to contraception and abortion. This is the result of them emphasizing personal autonomy as a means of resisting existing structures. However, they can also be against abortion if they see the unborn as being deserving of care and protection.

POLITICS THROUGH AN ELEPHANT LENS

Examples of the contrasting views of Liberal and Conservative Elephants using current and historical examples, both big and small.

In the following sections, we will examine various historical and contemporary examples through the lens of Elephant Theory to understand how the two major strains interact. From history, we will explore the cases of China and Japan, focusing on the critical decisions their elephants made and the resulting consequences. We will then analyze the rising tide of populism worldwide, using Germany and Donald Trump as examples. Additionally, we will discuss how Conservative and Liberal Elephants approach issues such as climate change, free speech and censorship, and DEI (Diversity, Equity, and Inclusion) policies. Finally, we will conclude by examining corporate culture and how the dominance of Liberal Elephants has influenced the Walt Disney Corporation and one of its major franchises, Star Wars.

CHINA

In China, Conservative Elephants reigned supreme,
with disastrous results.

For much of its history, China was the world's leading civilization, known for innovations such as writing, paper, and gunpowder. Its immense size and relative political stability contributed to this dominance. This legacy, still relatively recent in historical terms, remains a key aspect of China's national identity and self-perception. To Chinese nationalists, China's natural position in the world is as the "Middle Kingdom," the civilization around which all others revolve. However, at a crucial moment in its history, China turned inward and missed significant global developments that allowed other nations to surpass it. This inward turn was driven by the dominance of China's Conservative Elephants. As a result, China lost its position as the "Middle Kingdom" and has been grappling with the consequences of this shift ever since.

The height of Chinese influence occurred during the Ming Dynasty, from 1368 to 1644. During this period, China engaged in significant maritime exploration, most notably through the voyages of Admiral Zheng He between 1405 and 1433. Chinese trade and influence extended as far as the Middle East and Africa.

However, after Zheng He's expeditions, the Ming Dynasty shifted towards a more isolationist policy. This shift was due to the high costs of the voyages, internal political struggles, and the belief that China was so large that it didn't need external trade. The central government dismantled the fleet in favour of maintaining internal stability and defence. This very Conservative Elephant policy continued under the Qing Dynasty (1644–1912), as its conservative rulers were extremely wary of foreign influence, particularly through trade. The Qing restricted foreign trade and influence by limiting access to the port of Guangzhou (Canton).

China's policy of isolation was a result of Conservative Elephant thinking. The stability and social cohesion gained from this defensive approach allowed China to maintain its position as the world's leading civilization for a time. However, its complete lack of openness to foreign ideas caused it to miss out on two major developments: the

Enlightenment and the Industrial Revolution. While China focused inward, these ideas swept through Europe and transformed its societies. Eventually, China woke up to a world where every Western nation had surpassed it in terms of science and technology. Beginning with the First Opium War, China endured what became known as the "Century of Humiliation." During this period, China suffered a series of military defeats and was forced to accept humiliating treaties that ceded territory to various Western powers. By playing it safe, China had unknowingly allowed other nations to surpass it, suffering consequences that continue to affect the country to this day.

The lesson China teaches Conservative Elephants is that in their quest to maintain their herd's integrity, they must remain aware of what is happening beyond their borders, lest the world passes them by. Liberal Elephants, whose core evolutionary instinct is to seek out the different and the new, do not suffer from this myopia. Most new ideas, untested by time and reality, fail. However, a few are successful, and the Enlightenment and the Industrial Revolution certainly fall into that category. In this case, both China and the world would have been far better off if China had listened to its Liberal Elephants.

JAPAN

Like China, Japan experienced its own period of isolation, and for similar reasons. Japan's Conservative Elephants, embodied by the Tokugawa shogunate, were concerned about the influence of European powers and the spread of Christianity. To maintain their authority and preserve traditional Japanese culture, Japan implemented the "Sakoku" policy, which severely restricted foreign trade and interaction. However, during a key moment, Japan's Conservative Elephants took a different approach than their Chinese counterparts by listening to their Liberal brethren. This decision placed Japan on a radically different path, helping the country avoid China's fate.

The moment of truth for Japan's Conservative Elephants came on July 8, 1853, when Commodore Matthew Perry and his black ships sailed into Edo Bay (now Tokyo Bay). The United States, a rising power, saw ending Japan's isolation as critical to its strategic interests. U.S. President Millard Fillmore believed that establishing a stronger relationship with Japan was essential and sent Perry with an offer he thought Japan couldn't refuse.

Perry used a combination of carrots and sticks to show Japan's Conservative Elephants the benefits of opening up to the West, particularly to America. As a "carrot," he set up a small steam locomotive on a track and demonstrated a telegraph to showcase the advantages of Western science. He also presented several gifts, including modern firearms, telescopes, and agricultural tools, to highlight the benefits of American manufacturing and trade. On the "stick" side, Perry's modern warships were clearly superior to Japan's wooden vessels. To drive this point home, Perry fired his cannons, destroying a small structure he had built for demonstration purposes. The choice couldn't have been more clear: would Japan embrace the benefits of Western trade or risk the power of Perry's cannons?

To Japan's Conservative Elephants, the superiority of Perry's Western ways was undeniable. Likely encouraged by their Liberal counterparts, a consensus emerged that continued isolation was no longer an option. If Japan wanted to avoid the fate of other Asian countries that had fallen under Western colonial rule and influence, such as China, it needed to modernize. When Perry returned in 1854 with an even larger fleet, the Japanese willingly signed what became known as the Treaty of Kanagawa. Japan's isolationist policy, along with the Tokugawa Shogunate that upheld it, came to an end, and Emperor Meiji was restored to power. This marked the beginning of the Meiji Restoration, a period of intense modernization and Westernization in Japan. The country rapidly industrialized, adopting Western practices in military power, civil society, and education. By the late 19th and early 20th centuries, Japan had emerged as a major industrial and military power on the global stage.

Japan's elephant story demonstrates that Conservative Elephants can embrace change when convinced that failing to do so could endanger the herd.

GERMAN POPULISM

Why Germany's Liberal Elephants can't understand why the "right" is rising.

Elite Liberal Elephants around the world are concerned by what they see as an inexplicable surge of "populism" or "far-right" politics. In Germany, this has taken shape with the rise of the political party known as Alternative for Germany (AfD). The AfD is gaining political strength because it is addressing herd issues that Liberal Elephants are evolutionarily incapable of recognizing as legitimate. When these "herd issues" go unaddressed, a party of Conservative Elephants will inevitably emerge to fill the void. With their binary thinking, Liberal Elephants quickly categorize these challengers as "bad" and use every means to suppress them, except for addressing the underlying issues that caused them to rise in the first place. They instinctively reach for power, employing strategies of censorship and smear campaigns. However, because these tactics fail to address the legitimate concerns of Conservative Elephants, they inevitably backfire. Let's explore some of the herd issues the AfD is addressing and why Germany's Liberal Elephants are so baffled by its success.

RISING NATIONALISM AND EUROSKEPTICISM

Across Europe, there is a growing sense that harmful policies are being imposed by supranational bodies, such as the EU or UN, without any input or control from citizens. These institutions are overwhelmingly composed of Liberal Elephants, as they were designed to exercise power through top-down governance. Liberal Elephants champion these supranational organizations because, evolutionarily, they view issues in terms of problems and solutions and are confident they know what needs to be done. As a result, they have no qualms about imposing their global "solutions" over the national will of the people. Conservative Elephants, who live in these countries, increasingly resent this—especially when these "solutions" create stress within their herd. They respond by demanding a voice through their national representatives. This skepticism of supranational entities and the power they arrogantly wield fuels nationalist parties like the AfD. This is why at AfD rallies, you will often see the German flag (representing the nation or herd), while those opposing them display universal flags like Free Palestine or LGBTQ rights.

IMMIGRATION AND REFUGEES

One of the major policies that Conservative Elephants feel is being imposed on their countries by powerful elites is the issue of immigration and refugees. Increasing numbers of European citizens believe that immigration, both legal and illegal, is out of control. Poll after poll shows that the indigenous populations do not support this, and, worse, they feel powerless to stop it. No matter who they vote for, the issue persists, and their concerns are ignored. According to Elephant Theory, what's going on?

"Diversity is our strength" is the mantra of Liberal Elephants, who dominate international organizations such as the UN, EU, and national bureaucracies. In reality, this is an illusion, but an evolutionarily necessary one. Liberal Elephants see all elephants as the same and do not recognize the qualities that bind a herd or nation together. This is why, when given power, they see no problem in increasing immigration with elephants from very different herds. However, as they are constantly tearing down and demeaning the history and values of their existing cultures and nations, they never stop to ask themselves what these new elephants are going to join. What is going to bind this herd together? Once again, a major blind spot for Liberal Elephants is that they take the existing social fabric for granted. This is why more British Muslims reportedly have joined ISIS than the British Army, and why second and third-generation Muslims are often more radical than their parents. Why would anyone join the fabric of British society when Liberal Elephants have worked so hard to convince them it was terrible to begin with? Additionally, there is a suspicion that more devious Liberal Elephants favour increased immigration as a way to weaken nation-states, the main opponents of their globalist vision.

Conservative Elephants are focused on the complex and delicate social fabric of their herd, whether it be their community, city, or nation. They believe in the value of the existing diversity between nations. Whether it is Japan, China, America, or Germany, each nation has its own unique culture, history, and identity. Conservative Elephants do not mind when an ethnic enclave of new immigrants forms in their city. However, if the enclave grows so rapidly that it starts to dominate the city, the indigenous Conservative Elephants begin to feel alarmed. This concern intensifies when the new arrivals have radically different religious, cultural, or customary backgrounds. Conservative Elephants instinctively understand that "diversity is our strength" is a fallacy and that the more diverse a herd becomes, the more likely it is to fracture. The working class in these countries is the first to experience these issues. Meanwhile, wealthy Liberal Elephants, jet-setting around the world to attend climate conferences while sending their children to private schools, are largely insulated from these realities—at least for a time.

Conservative Elephants are not against immigration, as long as it is managed, controlled, and done for the benefit of the existing population. Their mantra, "unity is our strength," allows for immigration, provided that new arrivals unite around the higher principles of the culture. What made Western civilization unique, beginning with the ancient Greeks, was the idea that anyone could be accepted as a citizen if they embraced values that transcended race, culture, or religion. By accepting these values, it was possible to become Hellene, to become Greek. America, with its melting pot, is the modern equivalent of this ancient idea. Conservative Elephants favour a system where immigrants bring the best of their cultures and blend it with the best of the existing nation. This process, however, takes time and must be done carefully. Increasing numbers of Germans feel that the current immigration system is not being handled slowly, carefully, or with their interests in mind. This sentiment fuels the rise of nationalist and populist parties like the AfD.

ECONOMIC CONCERNS AND CLIMATE CHANGE

The working classes across the Western world are facing immense pressure due to the rising cost of living. To them, it seems that the rich are getting richer while they struggle just to stay afloat. One of the main reasons for this is the use of fiat currencies, which subtly rob the population for the benefit of the 1%. This destructive process is real but falls outside the scope of this book (for more on the topic, consider reading *What Has Government Done to Our Money?* by Murray Rothbard). Another major factor, however, is the policies that Liberal Elephants are dogmatically pursuing in the name of climate change.

The "fight" against climate change has become the modern left's global religion. It is such a significant issue that it deserves its own section, which we will discuss shortly. In Germany, Liberal Elephants are implementing "green energy" policies aimed at theoretically helping in the battle against climate change. However, the practical outcome of these policies is that cheap and reliable energy sources (fossil fuels) are being replaced by more expensive and less reliable ones. Since energy powers everything, this has led to rising costs everywhere. This demonstrates how Liberal Elephants often focus on "fixing" a single variable without considering the broader consequences. They prioritize the global issue over the well-being of the herd.

Opposition to these herd-crushing policies is what fuels the rise of Conservative Elephant parties like the AfD.

Concerns about immigration, national identity, sovereignty, climate policy, and the cost of living are all herd issues that Liberal Elephants struggle to perceive. This is why they find it difficult to address these concerns and often resort to censorship and name-calling toward those who raise them. However, this only highlights how out of touch elite Liberal Elephants are with the general population, further widening the political divide. It's reminiscent of a bad episode of *Star Trek,* where the crew of the Enterprise is threatened by a populist energy cloud. The Liberal Elephants in command order it to be blasted with the phasers of censorship and smears. To their horror, the energy cloud only grows stronger, feeding on the phasers' energy while expanding in power. In a real episode of *Star Trek*, the crew would stop firing immediately and have Mr. Spock analyze the cloud to develop a better strategy. Unfortunately, none of us are perfectly rational, and we don't have access to Mr. Spock. As a result, they continue firing their phasers until the cloud grows so large that it threatens to overwhelm them. This is what is happening in Europe right now, as various Liberal Elephants are forced to admit they underestimated the importance of migration, social stability, and the cost of living crisis.

TRUMP DERANGEMENT SYNDROME

For Liberal Elephants the world over, no one epitomizes their darkest populist fears than Donald Trump.

Like the rest of the Western world, America is experiencing a rising tide of nationalist populism. What makes the American version unique, however, is that it has manifested in the figure of one man—Donald J. Trump. Interestingly, Trump is also seemingly despised by a large portion of establishment Conservatives. At various points, both political lineages have tried to stop him, but because neither truly understands the forces that drive his popularity, their efforts have proven as futile as Elmer Fudd's attempts to catch Bugs Bunny. Why is this?

Throughout his life, Donald Trump has been a dealmaker rather than an ideologue. Essentially a New York Democrat, he worked with both parties to gain wealth and power. He is a man of both significant flaws and notable talents. One of these talents is his ability to sense the issues that resonate with the public and speak directly to them. In fact, he seems almost incapable of doing otherwise, as the thoughts that come into his head often travel to his mouth at lightning speed. This gives him a sense of authenticity that sharply contrasts with the carefully scripted, poll-tested responses of most professional politicians. It also makes him the ideal vessel to reflect the neglected concerns that fuel populist movements.

The populist herd issues that Donald Trump picked up on in his initial campaign for the presidency were as follows:

- America is involved in too many stupid wars and the Iraq war, in particular, was a disaster.
- The middle class is being hollowed out and foreign governments, particularly China, are getting away with murder. The Washington establishment is more interested in working for their masters in Corporate America than the people.
- Illegal immigration is out of control and America needs to build a wall (which Mexico will pay for).

Why did both branches of the establishment react with such revulsion to this man and his message? From an evolutionary perspective, each had its reasons. Let's begin with the conservative branch.

Establishment Conservative Elephants value the herd-preserving principles of loyalty, authority, and sanctity. When Donald Trump attacked George Bush and the Iraq War, he was challenging the herd's values of loyalty and authority. Instinctively, they saw this as a betrayal. However, this was also a key part of his appeal, as most establishment Conservative Elephants are unaware of how out of touch they are. Conservative Elephants also tend to view the political process as sacred, which is why they are more likely to elevate the Constitution and Bill of Rights as almost holy documents. They believe in the system and expect certain behavior within it. When you enter the house of a Conservative Elephant, they expect you to take off your shoes and not disturb anything. Donald Trump doesn't do this. This is why establishment Conservative Elephants treated him like an unwelcome guest who tracks mud into the house while knocking over your grandmother's urn. Trump's behavior offends establishment Conservative Elephants because they see his very presence as degrading a system they deeply value. These are the core moral objections of the Never Trumpers: loyalty, authority, and sanctity—Donald J. Trump offends each of these in some way.

If Trump exasperates Conservative Elephants, he outright torments their Liberal siblings in both media and politics. What drives them nearly to madness is that their unconstrained view of human nature is directly challenged when Trump criticizes illegal immigration. Trump's crudeness makes it feel like a personal, emotional attack. What's even more infuriating is that, despite the liberal political and media classes attacking him with their usual playbook of accusations (sexism, racism, homophobia, etc.), none of these labels seemed to affect him. Unlike the hapless Mitt Romney, who took their accusations seriously, Trump fires back without hesitation. Worse still, through his mastery of Twitter, he was able to bypass their top-down corporate media system and only seemed to grow stronger from their attacks. Despite mounting evidence that blasting the populist Trump movement with everything they had wasn't working, they continued to double down on this failed strategy. Evolutionarily, they could do no other, as their focused moral matrix prevents them from seeing the concerns Trump was addressing as legitimate.

With their attacks failing spectacularly and their inability to recognize the herd issues fuelling the Trump phenomenon as legitimate, deep-state Liberal Elephants chose to weaponize the legal system against him. Once again, their evolutionary binary nature betrayed them. Trump supporters believe that "The System" (not incorrectly) is rigged against them for the benefit of the powerful. When that same system is turned on their champion, it doesn't delegitimize Trump but the state itself. This is why Trump's rallying cries of "draining the swamp" and "In reality, they're not after me, they're after you. I'm just in the way" resonate so deeply. In their righteousness, Liberal Elephants are quite comfortable wielding the ring of power. However, their focused moral makeup prevents them from seeing the downsides of doing so. The re-election of Donald Trump may well be the result.

THE LEFT'S RELIGION - CLIMATE CHANGE

How Earth worship became the one true faith of Liberal Elephants worldwide

Few issues ignite more passion in Liberal Elephants than climate change. They speak about it in almost apocalyptic terms, warning that if we don't repent and make sacrifices to the carbon god, the world will literally end in 10 years. Variations of this belief are constantly espoused by Liberal Elephants at all levels. Alexandria Ocasio-Cortez, for example, stated that the world would end in 12 years if we didn't address climate change (she said this in 2019). Canadian Prime Minister Justin Trudeau has called climate change "the challenge of our generation." Liberal Elephants have been expressing similar sentiments for the past 40 years. Why is this? The reason isn't "science," but evolution. Climate change fits like a glove over their focused moral matrix and tickles their erogenous zones like no other. Here's why.

The Care/Harm axis is the most powerful value in the moral matrix of Liberal Elephants. They apply it universally, extending concern not only to their own herd but to elephants all over the world. This is why climate change fits so perfectly into their worldview—it allows them to rationalize that addressing it will help the poor in places like Africa, for example. Due to their evolutionary makeup, they do not see the trade-offs involved. They cannot even entertain the possibility that Africans might benefit far more from greater access to the cheap and reliable energy that fossil fuels provide. The most extreme climate change advocates elevate the Earth itself to the level of the sacred, viewing humanity and its civilization as the problem. This mindset gives rise to concepts like "Net Zero" and "Zero Impact." Although they will rarely admit it, often because they are unaware of it, they are opposed to the flourishing of humanity if it has any impact on Mother Earth.

Climate change also aligns perfectly with Liberal Elephants' universal perspective on the Liberty/Oppression axis. They can easily frame it as an oppressive system created by big oil, one they believe they can readily dismantle. Due to their binary good/bad thinking, Liberal Elephants never doubt their ability to make changes to gigantic complicated systems for the better.

The final axis that Liberal Elephants prioritize is Fairness/Cheating, and once again, climate change fits seamlessly. They perceive it as a global system where the rich countries exploit the poor. Similarly, they rationalize their concern for climate change in terms of intergenerational fairness, believing that failure to make sacrifices now will negatively affect future generations.

Due to their evolutionary makeup, no issue fits the moral matrix of Liberal Elephants quite like climate change. It is a broad, universal problem involving a large, systemic challenge they believe they can easily solve. It's like catnip to them. Conservative Elephants, with their more complex moral makeup, are not so sure.

Due to the constrained vision imposed by their moral matrix, Conservative Elephants have a more nuanced view of the issue. They are fully aware of how difficult it is to maintain a herd and recognize that the real world is filled with trade-offs rather than simple problems and solutions. To Conservative Elephants, modern civilization (the herd) is a miracle largely built on the availability of cheap, reliable, and plentiful energy provided by fossil fuels. Taking this for granted and discarding it to reduce a single variable is, in their view, reckless and potentially catastrophic. When they consider the issues facing the global poor, they do not attribute them solely to the all-encompassing boogeyman of climate change. Instead, they see a multitude of variables at play, including poor policy choices that have restricted access to the prosperity that cheap, reliable fossil fuels can offer. They also suspect that the billions spent on climate change initiatives might be better allocated to programs like alleviating malnutrition in Africa. Conservative Elephants see the real world as a complex place that defies simple solutions.

Conservative Elephants are keenly aware of how difficult it is to predict the future due to the inherent complexity of reality. Liberal Elephants justify their schemes based on computer models and call it science. Conservative Elephants are extremely skeptical of these predictions, as models—no matter how complex—always fall far short of accurately reflecting reality. The true way to test models and theories is against real-world outcomes. When they do this, they find that the list of predictions made by computer models and environmental doomsayers is long and largely inaccurate. For example:

- In 1988 climate activists predicted that the Maldive Islands will be underwater by 2018 (they're not)
- In 1989 climate activists predicted that the New York City West Side Highway will be underwater by 2019 (it's not)

- In 2000 climate activists predicted that snowfall will be a thing of the past (it's not)
- In 2005 climate activists predicted Manhattan will be underwater by 2015 (it's not)
- In 2008 climate activists Al Gore predicted that the Arctic will be ice free by 2013 (it's not)
- In 2011 climate activists predicted in the Washington Post that Cherry Blossoms will soon bloom in the winter (they don't)

The focused moral matrix of Liberal Elephants causes them to ignore these realities. They see problems and solutions, not trade-offs. As a result, they sweep these predictive failures under the rug when they threaten their beliefs.

Some Conservative Elephants attempt to find common ground with their Liberal counterparts by promoting nuclear power. Although they have serious reservations about whether climate change is the apocalyptic crisis that Liberal Elephants claim, nuclear energy has the potential to replace fossil fuels by being superior (more reliable and cheaper) with no carbon emissions. Some Liberal Elephants, once they understand this potential, embrace it. Others, however, do not. The reason is the same as why they ignore their failed computer model predictions: climate change is their religion, and heretical facts are not to be entertained.

As mentioned previously, some Liberal Elephants extend their belief in the Care/Harm axis to the Earth itself. Most religious worldviews, such as Christianity, view the structure of the universe as God, Man, Earth. Extreme Liberal Elephants, who often do not believe in a higher power, place the natural world—Earth—above Man. This is why they do not support nuclear power. Their goal is not to reduce carbon emissions but to reduce humanity's impact on the world. To them, humanity itself is the original sin, and reducing its impact—even to the point of destroying civilization—is their spiritual doctrine. This is why, at its most extreme, climate change is not only a religion but a dangerous one.

FREE SPEECH & CENSORSHIP

*Both Elephants can censor, albeit for
different reasons.*

Freedom of speech is considered an essential civil right in most of the West. It is seen as a foundational principle vital to maintaining individual liberty and civil society. In the West, this civil right was born during the Enlightenment to give the common man a way of challenging existing authority. For example, if one wanted to challenge institutions like the Church or the monarchy, freedom of speech was essential. Sunlight is the best disinfectant, and good ideas, if given the space to breathe, can overcome the lies of corrupt establishments. In terms of Elephant Theory, both evolutionary strains support the concept of free speech. However, when this principle clashes with their moral instincts, both Elephants will often abandon it, though for different reasons. Here's why.

Conservative Elephants' commitment to free speech weakens when faced with speech that challenges the integrity of the herd. This is why conservatives are often in favour of censoring works they consider pornographic. Conservative Elephants view pornography as a form of free speech that undermines the integrity of the herd by attacking the sanctity of women, motherhood, and marriage. These "herd values" are considered critical and sacred for protecting and maintaining the community. In their zeal, extreme Conservative Elephants can fall prey to attempting to ban great works of art for the same reasons. Herd integrity is also at the root of Conservative Elephants' objections to certain types of music, particularly rock and rap, as these genres are seen as subverting the sanctity of family values and the loyalty and authority of institutions such as the police or the nation-state.

Conservative Elephants' attempts to ban books are also rooted in censoring ideas seen as threatening to the integrity of the herd. Pornography falls into this category, but so do ideas that weaken institutional loyalty and authority. One example was the attempt by Conservative Elephants to ban the book *Catch-22* in various school districts during the 1960s. In times of war, such as the Vietnam War, Conservative Elephants become hyper-aware of any speech that may undermine the herd's ability to fight. *Catch-22,* with its anti-war sentiment and portrayal of wartime leadership as incompetent, corrupt, and self-serving, triggered significant alarm within the Conservative Elephant's moral framework.

In summary, Conservative Elephants' attempts to censor are typically aimed at suppressing speech seen at threatening to the integrity of the herd they belong to.

Liberal Elephants often express support for free speech in theory, as they see it as a useful tool for challenging pre-existing systems they view as oppressive or unjust. In practice, however, all but the most farsighted and principled Liberal Elephants can falter on the question of free speech due to their unconstrained nature and binary thinking. Seeing issues in terms of good or bad, right or wrong, with no nuance, easily leads them down a path of censorship. Of course, they are open to hearing all sides—but why hear all sides when one side is so obviously wrong? This led William F. Buckley to observe:

"Liberals claim to want to give a hearing to other views, but then are shocked and offended to discover that there are other views."

This is why the censorship that Liberal Elephants engage in is often more harmful and dangerous than that of their conservative counterparts. To remain true to their evolutionary belief that diversity is our strength and we are all the same, they are willing to censor speech that threatens this belief, even when it is true. Facts don't matter when they challenge evolutionary convictions.

An example of the milder end of the Liberal Elephant's censorship spectrum is trigger warnings. The reason for this is that great literature, like The Great Gatsby or the works of Dostoevsky, portrays the world as it truly is—warts and all. Depictions of violence and man's inhumanity to man do not align with their evolutionary worldview that all elephants are inherently good. This is further compounded by the fact that most of us have been raised in a time of relative peace and prosperity. We have not experienced events that highlight the darker side of the human condition, such as World War II, the Great Depression, or the Holocaust. Books that depict this harsh reality can cause psychological discomfort, which is why Liberal Elephants promote trigger warnings at best and, at worst, outright book banning.

At the more extreme end of the Liberal Elephant's censorship spectrum is their willingness to ban and shut down speakers with whom they disagree. Jordan Peterson, Ayaan Hirsi Ali, and Riley Gaines have all experienced this on college campuses, which are often considered bastions of free speech. The reason these young Liberal Elephants respond this way is that these speakers are addressing "herd issues" that their focused moral matrix does not recognize.

Their good/bad binary thinking then takes over, allowing them to justify shutting down speakers they disagree with while still seeing themselves as "the good guys." They often defend their actions by declaring, "Hate speech is not free speech," with "hate" often being defined as opinions they don't agree with or understand.

One of the most striking examples of this type of censorship is that experienced by scholar and researcher Heather Mac Donald. Mac Donald has written works such as *The War on Cops* and *The Diversity Delusion*, books that directly challenge the focused morality of Liberal Elephants. In *The War on Cops*, for example, she challenged the entire Black Lives Matter narrative, which claims that Black Americans are victimized by a police force riddled with systemic racism. Instead, she argued that racial disparities in crime rates result from deeper social and economic issues within the Black community itself. Essentially, and perhaps without realizing it, she is arguing that the issues facing the Black community stem from "herd issues" rather than blaming top-down oppressive systems favoured by Liberal Elephants. Once again, Heather Mac Donald's arguments are rooted in a moral matrix that Liberal Elephants, particularly young ones, cannot perceive or engage with. This is why they respond with such fury, doing everything in their power to shut her down while calling her every toxic name in the book. In the past, this has included vandalizing buildings and preventing people from attending her lectures. In the name of "anti-fascism," Liberal Elephants will, ironically, engage in some of the most fascist actions imaginable.

When it comes to free speech, both Elephants will express their support. However, both will waver when that speech challenges the core values of their respective moralities. For Conservative Elephants, this involves speech that challenges their "herd values" of sanctity, authority, and loyalty. On the other hand, Liberal Elephants will censor speech that challenges their "unconstrained view" that everyone is inherently good and the same, and that all problems are the result of systems they believe they can change.

DIVERSITY, EQUITY AND INCLUSION

*The Mantra of Liberal Elephants Heralds The End
of Civilizations.*

"Diversity is our strength" is the most sacred belief held by Liberal Elephants. Due to their biological need to be open to others, Liberal Elephants must believe that all people are the same, regardless of race, culture, or sex—it does not matter. Therefore, they conclude that any perceived inequality must be the result of an unjust system. Furthermore, due to their binary thinking, they believe they have the wisdom to change that system easily. In modern times, this principle has led to the doctrine known as DEI, or Diversity, Equity, and Inclusion. It is the logical outcome of following a false premise to a disastrous conclusion. Since it is based on a falsehood, it often harms the very people it was meant to help while undermining any institution that adopts its creed.

The problem with the Liberal Elephant's belief in equality is that it is a delusion, albeit an evolutionarily necessary one. The harsh reality of the world is that nothing is equal, nothing is fair, and nothing is the same. As Thomas Sowell points out, the Zaire River in Africa actually carries more water than the Mississippi. However, while the Mississippi's riverbed declines at a steady rate of 4 inches per mile, the Zaire is full of spectacular waterfalls and cascades. This is great for tourism but a disaster for economic development. The Zaire and Mississippi are both rivers, but they are not the same. Likewise, most tornadoes in the world occur in a region of the U.S. known as "Tornado Alley." Tornadoes are not evenly distributed throughout the world. Nothing in the natural world is "equal" or "the same."

As it is with nature, so it is with the human race. Simply look at a random group of people walking down the street, and it is obvious that they are not equal. This does not mean they shouldn't be treated with respect, but they are not the same. I am not Michael Jordan. You are not Taylor Swift. The truth is that most of us are not even equal to ourselves throughout the day. Some people are very productive in the morning ("morning people"), while others are not. The idea that people are essentially the same and interchangeable is a necessary biological delusion that Liberal Elephants must rationalize in order to be so open to genetic diversity. The problem with this delusion is that it is divorced from reality. When people try to warp the real world of flesh and blood to fit this idea, disastrous unintended consequences occur.

One example of this is the push for diversity on college campuses through the policy of affirmative action. Liberal Elephants look at the dearth of Black students at MIT, for example, and conclude that this is the result of systemic discrimination. It must be so, as their biological imperative forces them to see everyone as inherently good and the same. Conservative Elephants look at the same issue and suspect that "herd issues" are a more likely culprit. Does the culture value education? Did the students come from stable families? How hard are the students working? How many students are in the pipeline that might attend MIT to begin with? Evolutionarily, Liberal Elephants cannot see these factors and therefore institute policies like affirmative action to correct what they see as an unjust system. The result of this rejection of reality is that promising Black students are placed in situations where they are set up to fail. As Thomas Sowell points out, Black students attending MIT were in the top 10% of math students in the country. However, this placed them in the bottom 10% at MIT. Likewise, when Sowell taught at Cornell, the average Black student's SAT score was in the 75th percentile, while the average White student's score was in the 99th. The result of this mismatch was that half of the Black students were on academic probation. The reality is that people come from different backgrounds, have different abilities, and learn at different rates. By placing Black students in academic institutions for which they are unsuited, Liberal Elephants do them a great disservice by setting them up to fail. They wind up sacrificing promising Black students on their altar of "diversity."

This mismatching of merit and abilities in the name of DEI is not only weakening our universities and causing great harm to their students, but it is also undermining every other institution that our society relies on. Functioning civilizations are not built on bumper sticker slogans like "Diversity is our strength," but on universal values of merit and competence. "Unity is our strength"—unity on accepted standards—is what keeps elephant herds together and thriving.

THE DESECRATION OF DISNEY & STAR WARS

*Why "Diversity" Destroys Shared Culture and
Beloved Franchises*

Modern Hollywood is a creative and financial dumpster fire. It is a prime example of an institution compromised to the point of self-destruction by the dominance of Liberal Elephants. Strategically, this is happening due to Tinseltown's adherence to the false doctrine of DEI. Tactically, it is occurring because the bread and butter of the entertainment industry is to entertain. This cannot be done without compelling stories, and the art of storytelling is, as we shall see, a conservative act. If Hollywood wishes to reverse its descent into irrelevance, it must learn to embrace its Conservative Elephants and their "herd values" quickly. Failure to do so may well seal its doom.

The most dramatic example of Hollywood's strategic failure may be the Walt Disney Company. Since its inception, Disney has been known as a master storyteller, consistently producing hit after hit. Its animation studios, particularly revitalized by the acquisition of Pixar in 2006, became synonymous with must-see cinema. Pixar delivered major successes like *Toy Story 3 & 4*, *Inside Out*, and *Coco*. During this period, Disney Animation also thrived with hits like *Frozen*, *Zootopia*, and *Moana*. In recent years, however, both studios seem to have lost their magic touch. Pixar has produced forgettable films such as *Turning Red* and *Lightyear*, while Disney Animation has released flops like *Strange World* and, most notably, *Wish*. What happened?

The decline of Disney animation is a microcosm of Hollywood itself, and the culprit is the same: the false mantra of "Diversity is our strength" and its offspring, DEI. In Disney's case, this trend accelerated with the departure of John Lasseter in 2018 under a cloud of questionable #MeToo allegations. As detailed in Film Threat's *The D-Files*, Lasseter's exit led to the rise of Jennifer Lee as Chief Creative Officer. Lee, a champion of diversity, believed the studio was too white and male. She set a goal of increasing diversity by, among other things, ensuring that 50% of animators were female. This shift warped the corporate culture, to the point where experienced animators, who were predominantly white and male, were viewed as "pale and stale." They were made to feel uncomfortable as junior animators, with far less experience and training, were promoted over them and given positions of power. Seeing the writing on the wall, many of these talented animators began to leave. But who cares? "Diversity is our strength," right?

Wrong. In the real world, "Unity is our strength," meaning adherence to universal standards of artistic ability and excellence. The reason that so many of the master animators at Disney were white and male is because, for whatever reason, that was the demographic most interested in the art and willing to put in the time at Cal Arts, USC, and UCLA. For them, Disney was the dream, and the animation departments of these and other schools provided a pipeline of talent that Disney could draw from. Once again, Conservative Elephants understand that reality is messy and complex. If you attempt to use the ring of power to impose quotas based on secondary characteristics, you do so at the expense of talent and ability. This is the trade-off you will be making, whether your moral framework recognizes it or not. Hiring individuals whose background was in Tumblr animation will come at a cost. In this case, it resulted in films such as *Wish*, which the studio had high hopes for but failed spectacularly. After a string of underperforming creative failures, Jennifer Lee "stepped down" as Chief Creative Officer. With the talent exodus Disney experienced under her leadership, it will be some time before Disney can reacquire the standards of excellence it was once known for—if it is even possible.

As bad as Hollywood is failing due to the strategic failures of DEI, it is at the tactical level of storytelling where the most damage has been done. The bedrock on which the Hollywood dream factory was built is the ability to tell compelling and inspiring stories. This is a skill that Tinseltown has seemingly lost. Part of the reason, DEI, has already been mentioned. However, the more fundamental reason is that the art of storytelling is rooted in the conservative moral matrix. As Margaret Thatcher once noted, "The facts of life are conservative," and this applies to storytelling as well. The evolutionary false (but necessary) beliefs of Liberal Elephants—that all people are "the same" and that any differences are the result of systemic oppression—fail to capture the totality of the human experience. The reality is that we are all different, with different backgrounds and different abilities. What unites us is our shared journey through life. In classic storytelling, this is known as the hero's journey, and although the particulars of each of our journeys are unique, the arc of the story is the same. It is this reality that great stories—the stories that truly matter—

speak to. They provide templates and clues for how you, too, can rise to the occasion and become better than you are.

As the Critical Drinker points out (see his video essay on *Why Do We Need Heroes*), stories such as Achilles and Hector in *The Iliad* or Saint George and the Dragon provided these templates in the past. In the modern world, our heroes come from the realm of comic books, movies, and TV. Whoever our heroes are, their role in inspiring us remains the same. If two little hobbits can find the courage to carry the ring of power to Mordor, perhaps you can find the courage to start that business, stand up for the cause you believe in, or follow your passions wherever they lead. It is not just Gilgamesh who exists in *The Hero With a Thousand Faces*, but you as well.

One example of a film franchise that drew deeply from our shared well of human experience is *Star Wars*. The reason the original three films were such a worldwide phenomenon is that they reflected the universal conservative values of the hero's journey through the character of Luke Skywalker. We first meet Luke as a whiny teenager who recoils from the mundane responsibilities of farm life while yearning for something more. He then hears the call to adventure through his encounters with the droids R2-D2 and C-3PO and finds a mentor in Obi-Wan Kenobi. Luke crosses the threshold at the Mos Eisley Cantina and commits to his adventure by boarding the Millennium Falcon. Along the way, he is tested while meeting various allies and enemies. He completes his journey by destroying the Death Star and returns transformed. He began the story as a boy but is now a man.

The reason Luke's journey resonated with people everywhere is that it is universal. Everyone, at some point, has felt lost and wondered if they have the courage to make a change. Modern Hollywood, dominated by the moral matrix of Liberal Elephants, instinctively rejects the hero's journey. Their evolutionary makeup compels them to see everyone as the same and to dismiss the idea that individual initiative matters. This is why Liberal Elephants are so determined to "deconstruct" and tear down heroes from the past. It's also why Disney's *Star Wars* took such delight in destroying the legacies of Luke Skywalker and Han Solo—turning one into an infantile loser sucking at a space cow's teat and the other into a deadbeat dad.

Since they don't understand or respect the hero's journey, modern Hollywood "creatives" attempt to replace it in one of two ways. The first is through the self-insert, which means creating characters that do not inspire but instead reflect the writer's personal experience. One example of this is *Acolyte* showrunner Leslye Hedland, who stated that she didn't "see myself in shows," referring to LGBTQ characters. She went on to create *The Acolyte*, earning it the twin distinctions of being "the gayest *Star Wars* show ever" and also one of the lowest rated. The second way is through the "Girl Boss" phenomenon, a character who already has all the abilities she needs (and it is usually a woman) and only has to reject "the system" that had been limiting her to realize them. *Captain Marvel* is an example of this trope.

The real world is complicated, full of imperfect solutions and trade-offs. The reality is that only a fraction of your potential audience is LGBTQ, and only a fraction of that group wants to "see themselves" onscreen. Queer cinema has always existed, but it remains a niche. The extent to which this agenda can be pushed into the mainstream is limited, especially when those pushing it are not particularly talented to begin with. The same is true of the "Girl Boss" trope. The reality is that, as human beings, we all have strengths and weaknesses, and any effort to improve involves experiencing a form of the hero's journey. This is why the "Girl Boss" and similar clichés are championed mainly by political activists who rarely consume the products they promote. Neither trope resonates with nor inspires a general audience.

What does?

Twin Sun moments.

In Star Wars, there is an iconic scene early in the film where Luke silently watches the twin suns of Tatooine fade beneath the horizon. He feels lost, purposeless, and overwhelmed by a longing for something better. As John Williams' mesmerizing score washes over the audience, every one of them—regardless of race, class, or colour—can empathize with what Luke is feeling. We've all felt this way at some point in our lives and likely will again. It is this universal nature of the human experience that connects with people, and until Hollywood rediscovers its ability to unite us in our shared humanity, its slow-moving demolition will continue.

CONQUEST'S SECOND LAW

For Institutions to Thrive in the Long Term,
Conservative Elephants Are Key

Robert Conquest was a renowned historian and author. Through his speeches and writings he is known for formulating Conquest's Three Laws of Politics. They are:

Everyone is conservative about what they know best.

Any organization not explicitly right-wing sooner or later becomes left-wing.

The simplest way to explain the behaviour of any bureaucratic organization is to assume that it is controlled by a cabal of its enemies.

For our purposes the second law will be our focus. Although Conquest wasn't writing in the context of Liberal and Conservative Elephants he may well have been. It is hard not to see any organization or institution in the West that does not validate Conquest's hypothesis. From government bureaucracy (the deep state) to corporate media to the universities, every organization and institution we have has drifted left. Why does this occur?

Elephant Theory suggests two primary reasons. One is the Liberal Elephant belief in the equality of people—that we are all the same. Once they have sufficient numbers to control an institution, they begin to recruit elephants based on secondary characteristics such as race and sex rather than merit or the competence required for the institution's stated purpose. Allowing the liberal evolutionary value of "diversity" to trump the conservative value of merit and competence ("unity is our strength") inevitably undermines the institution.

The second reason is that Liberal Elephants, with their focused moral matrix and unconstrained views of human nature, do not recognize as legitimate the nuanced perspectives of their Conservative counterparts. This is why, instinctively, Liberal Elephants suppress conservative ideas and prevent Conservative Elephants from being hired in the first place. As day passes into night, the results of this process are as predictable as they are ruinous. Liberal Elephants come to dominate the institution, which then begins to fall apart as it loses its purpose. Consider the following examples.

UNIVERSITIES AND COLLEGES

In 1950, the average grade at Harvard was 2.5. Today, in 2024, it is 3.8. This phenomenon of grade inflation is the result of lowered standards that occur when the influence of Conservative Elephants wanes and the ethos of Liberal Elephants takes over. Combined with the fact that free speech is no longer protected on many college campuses, Ivy League degrees are no longer as valued or impressive as they may have once been.

BUSINESSES

"Get Woke, Go Broke" has become a well-known adage, describing how many established companies adopt messaging or policies that end up hurting their core business. Some examples:

Anheuser-Busch (Bud Light) – The core mission of Anheuser-Busch is to sell beer to men. In the past, they successfully did this by associating their brand with things men like, such as parties, fun, and attractive women. This strategy served them well. Then, in a move that seems nonsensical (but makes sense if you understand Elephant Theory), they turned their back on their traditional customers by launching a marketing campaign featuring transgender influencer Dylan Mulvaney. This led to a significant drop in sales, with Bud Light losing its position as the best-selling beer in the U.S.

Gillette – Like Anheuser-Busch, Gillette's customer base was predominantly men, which is why they targeted this demographic. One of their most successful campaigns centered on the theme "The best a man can get." This slogan, a reflection of Conservative Elephant values, celebrated masculinity and encouraged men to be their best (with the help of Gillette products, of course). However, when Liberal Elephants took over, they produced a campaign that felt more like a public service announcement about "toxic masculinity" than an advertising campaign. Instead of inspiring men, this ad seemed to attack them. As a result, Gillette reported significant financial losses.

Target – Target is a big-box retailer whose primary customer base consists of working-class Americans. In a nod to DEI, their Liberal Elephant CEO decided to partner with a designer associated with Satanism to promote Pride-related merchandise, including "tuck-friendly" swimwear and T-shirts with slogans like "Satan respects pronouns." The backlash against Target for this promotion was severe and led to a significant loss in market share for a period of time.

What all of these examples demonstrate is the truth of Robert Conquest's second law and what happens when

Liberal Elephants come to dominate institutions, including allegedly for-profit corporations. True to their evolutionary nature, they:

- *Fail to respect their existing customer base* – This is a result of the openness of Liberal Elephants, which causes them to ignore the social fabric of their existing herds.

- *See issues in binary terms of right and wrong as opposed to trade-offs* – Promoting trans-friendly products aimed at kids was "the right thing for socicty," according to a top Target executive. He was blind to the fact that a major part of Target's customer base increasingly has a negative view of trans issues, particularly when it involves accepting men in women's sports or pushing this ideology onto children.

- *See issues in terms of oppressive systems* – Gillette's commercial illustrated "toxic" behaviour as part of a system for which all men are responsible. This stems from their "everyone is the same" unconstrained philosophy, which views every problem as a result of systemic oppression. In contrast, the original Conservative Elephant ads emphasized that men are great and should strive to be the best they can be. Which do you think will sell more razors: the commercial saying "you suck, do better," or "you can be great"?

CORPORATE MEDIA

There are many reasons why corporate or legacy media is dying worldwide. One is that their economic models no longer work, and they are being outcompeted by smaller, more nimble competitors. Another reason is that they have become centralized and corporatized, fed by universities that produce only well-trained Liberal Elephants. Even if they wanted to, it is hard for them to challenge a system that literally raised them. This is why they are so prone to hoaxes such as the Russian Collusion Hoax, the Very Fine People Hoax, or the Hunter Biden Laptop is Russian Disinformation Hoax. Their biggest failure, however, may have been how willingly they became the mouthpiece of the Covid regime, never challenging any of its absurd policies. It is very difficult to challenge the establishment when you are part of it.

THE ENTERTAINMENT INDUSTRY

I've already talked about the fall of Disney but what is true for them is true of the entire entertainment industry, from films (Phase 4 of the Marvel Cinematic Universe) and television (*She-Hulk)* to comics (the American comic book industry is dead) and video games (*Concord*). All are now being produced by individuals who check certain favoured diversity checkboxes over talent and merit. This is the root of the mantra "Go Woke, Go Broke."

All of these institutions have become dominated by Liberal Elephants, and all have grown weaker as a result. They corroborate Conquest's hypothesis:

Any organization not explicitly right-wing sooner or later becomes left-wing.

If we were to rewrite Conquest's law through the lens of Elephant Theory it might look something like this:

Any institution that does not value and actively recruit Conservative Elephants will soon lose its power and purpose

The reality is that the Liberal Elephant philosophy of "Diversity is our Strength" is an evolutionarily necessary falsehood. For any herd, or organization, to thrive it must rally around the Conservative Elephant truth that "Unity is our Strength." This means adhering to the principles of:

Unity of standards

Unity in how we are treated

Unity in our pursuit of excellence.

Regardless of race, sex or creed.

Unity is our Strength

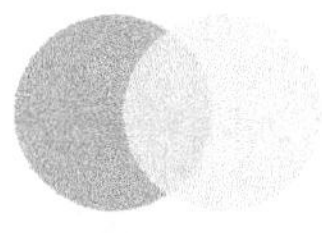

BONUS: WHEN ELEPHANTS STAMPEDE

I began this book by illustrating how the human brain is like a computer made up of a hierarchy of subconscious layers. They are:

- **Primal Instinct Layer** - Home of our oldest and most powerful primal urges, such as the will to survive and the desire to procreate.

- **Group Morality Layer** - The second most powerful layer is filled with instructions on how we should treat each other in service of our instinct layer.

- **Logic Reason Layer** - The most recent addition to our computer brain. It allows us to manipulate the world around us in ways that no other species can. The mistake people make is that they think this layer is in charge when in reality it is always in service of the first two subconscious drives.

This book is primarily concerned with how we deal with various issues and each other based on the instructions of the Group Morality Layer. I do want to briefly mention what happens when the most powerful drive we have, our Primal Instinct Layer, is activated by the most powerful fear we have, namely, the fear of death. When this happens to enough people an elephant stampede can happen which both Liberal and Conservative Elephants will participate in. During a stampede all norms of behaviour, including science and reason, will be thrown out the window. This is what occurred during the mass stampede of the Covid panic. This is why when clear-eyed commentators look back on that dark era of our history the most common theme is how nothing that was done made any sense. The reason for this is that they are attempting to use their Logic Reason Layer to rationalize actions rooted in the Primal Instinct Layer. This is why the majority of scientists turned on a dime to advocate for such CCP Fang Kong inspired nonsense as:

- 6 feet social distancing
- Masking
- Lockdowns

None of the policies were accepted before the panic. However, once a stampede starts due to the most powerful of primal fears (literally, the fear of death) scientists will join with the stampede and will rationalize any half-baked ritual that might offer some semblance of a plan. During a stampede, the first elephants to realize that something is off are a subset we have not discussed yet, Independent Elephants. Independent Elephants have the ability to separate themselves from the herd to get the big picture, including when the herd is heading towards a cliff. They can come from both Liberal and Conservative strains and from all parts of society. How effective the Independent Elephants are in waking up the stampeding herd determines how long the panic will go on.

In psychological terms, an elephant stampede is often referred to as an episode of mass hysteria or mass formation psychosis. As the stampede continues it can easily take a dark turn into a moral panic. A moral panic occurs when the stampeding herd identifies "the other" as a source of their fear. During the early stages of the covid panic a milder form of this can be seen in how the first Independent Elephants to question the Covid Regime's response, including scientists, were shouted down, ostracized and censored. Again, this response only makes sense in the context of a panicked herd running for its life. Science and reason had nothing to do with it. As the panic continues the stampeding herd will then shamefully look for scapegoats. It found them with the introduction of the experimental mRNA shots and the subsequent scapegoating of the unvaccinated. Once again, this behaviour cannot be explained or justified on the basis of science or reason. Like the internment of Japanese Canadians and Americans during World War II, it can only be understood in terms of a mass hysteria.

Currently I'm working on two books. *The Little Book of Elephant Theory* is the book you are currently reading and is primarily concerned with the implications of the Group Morality Layer of the human brain. The second book, however, is *The Little Book of Covid Red Pills*, and it is concerned with the Covid Panic that was driven by the Primal Instinct Layer. I'm planning on expanding both books into larger, more substantive works. I'm still in the planning stages for this, but for my planned *BIG Book of Elephant Theory* it will include:

1. More examples of how both Elephants deal with different issues and why
2. How Conservative Elephants can better frame issues to gain the support of their Liberal kin (and vice versa)
3. Ideas from you!

That last one is most important. If you like this book but have some ideas on territory you think I should cover in *The BIG Book of Elephant Theory*, feel free to shoot me an email at:

feedback@davidnordmark.ca

With respect to *The BIG Book of Covid Red Pills* it will delve deeper into the following topics in a unique way:

1. *Covid Stories* - How focusing on the single variable of "Covid Cases" caused so much collateral damage

2. *Censorship and Propaganda* - Examples of how and why the Covid Regime engaged in practices that no government body should (in a society that professes to be free, anyway)

3. *The Importance of Independent Elephants* - How societies rely on Independent Elephants to sound the alarm when the herd is running towards a cliff (I'll go into more detail on this important species.)

4. *The reality of "Experts"* - Throughout the panic people turned to "Experts" as if they were rational Mr. Spocks. This proved to be an illusion as most "Experts" are just as human as any of us and more prone to groupthink than most. In a stampede they will rationalize, not reason.

If you are interested in the first version of this book, you can get *The Little Book of Covid Red Pills* here:

RedPillCovid.com

Or from books2read (this has links to most of the major ebook retailers) here:

https://books2read.com/u/moJ2oJ

I also create videos on these and other topics under the moniker of "Experts Say" on YouTube, X and Rumble. Links to these can be found on my LinkTree here:

https://linktr.ee/ExpertsSay

In the meantime, I would like to thank you for taking the time to read my work and for any thoughts you might have.

Thank you for supporting my work,

My hand in yours,

Dave

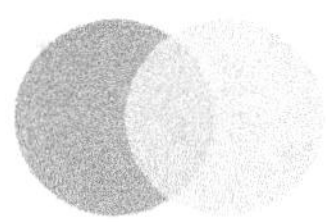

SELECTED BIBLIOGRAPHY

BOOKS

Adams, S. (2017). *Win Bigly - Persuasion In A World Where Facts Don't Matter*. Portfolio/Penguin.

Cialdini, R. B., Ph.D. (1984). *Influence - The Psychology of Persuasion*. Harper Collins.

Cialdini, R. B., Ph.D. (2016). *Pre-Suasion - A Revolutionary Way to Influence and Persuade*. Simon & Schuster.

Desmet, M. (2022). *The Psychology Of Totalitarianism*. Chelsea Green Publishing.

Haidt, J. (2013). *The Righteous Mind: Why Good People Are Divided by Politics and Religion*. Vintage.

MacIntyre, A. (2024). *The Total State: How Liberal Democracies Become Tyrannies*. Regnery.

Sowell, T. (2006). *A Conflict Of Visions - Ideological Origins of Political Struggles*. Basic Books.

NEWSPAPERS

Smith, J. (n.d.). *REVEALED: Target Pride collection includes bags and sweaters by Satan-loving trans designer who wants to 'burn down the cis-tem' - as backlash against retail giant grows*. DailyMail.com. https://www.dailymail.co.uk/news/article-12115573/Target-facing-boycott-Pride-collection-Satan-loving-designer.html

PODCASTS / VIDEO

[Film Threat]. (2023, December 22). *THE D-FILES CH. 1: THE DOWNFALL OF DISNEY & JOHN LASSETER* | Film Threat [Video]. YouTube. https://youtu.be/XEEeDvivN5c?si=V7bxBwj4ETEQcsiK

[Midnight's Edge]. (2024, June 3). *The Acolyte will DESTROY Star Wars FOREVER; Leslye Headland SET UP to Take The Fall!?* [Video]. YouTube. https://youtu.be/dURTaR357vg?si=FGDErZEPyIkWpO1P

[Midnight's Edge]. (2024, June 24). *The Acolyte and the Destruction of Star Wars Blame Game BEGINS* [Video]. YouTube. https://youtu.be/9ImsxYCW9FY?si=zSws7QAgCeXaM52C

[The Critical Drinker]. (2020, December 2). *Why Do We Need Heroes?* [Video]. YouTube. https://youtu.be/ow79eUHFhp0?si=PMDFdSlj770eODw